One World

THE HISTORY AND GOVERNMENT OF
South Asia

RACHAEL MORLOCK

PowerKiDS
press.

Published in 2021 by The Rosen Publishing Group, Inc.
29 East 21st Street, New York, NY 10010

First Edition

Editor: Caitie McAneney
Book Design: Seth Hughes

Photo Credits: Cover (top) SAKhanPhotography/Shutterstock.com; cover (bottom) Efired/Shutterstock.com; p. 5 Pyty/Shutterstock.com; p. 7 https://upload.wikimedia.org/wikipedia/commons/d/db/Site_Location_of_Mehrgarh.jpg; p. 8 Globe Turner, LLC/Getty Images; pp. 9, 10 DEA/G. NIMATALLAH/De Agostini/Getty Images; p. 11 DEA/W. BUSS/De Agostini/Getty Images; p. 12 MASSOUD HOSSAINI/AFP/Getty Images; p. 13 https://upload.wikimedia.org/wikipedia/commons/e/e5/Indo-Gangetic_Plain.en.png; p. 14 Malcolm P Chapman/Moment/Getty Images; p. 15 saiko3p/iStock/Getty Images Plus/Getty Images; p. 16 DEA/M. BORCHI/De Agostini/Getty Images; p. 18 Casper1774Studio/iStock/Getty Images Plus/Getty Images; p. 19 Heritage Images; p. 22 NurPhoto/Getty Images; p. 23 (top) Arterra/Universal Images Group/Getty Images; p. 23 (bottom) Frank Bienewald/LightRocket/Getty Images; p. 24 https://upload.wikimedia.org/wikipedia/commons/4/4d/Mughal-empire-map.jpg; p. 26 DEA PICTURE LIBRARY/De Agostini/Getty Images; p. 27 LUDOVIC MARIN/AFP/Getty Images; p. 29 Werner Forman/Hulton Fine Art Collection/Getty Images; pp. 30, 33 (top) Print Collector/Hulton Fine Art Collection/Getty Images; p. 31 UniversalImagesGroup/Getty Images; p. 32 Felice Beato/Hulton Archive/Getty Images; p.33 (bottom) Royal Geographical Society/Getty Images; p. 35 (top) Underwood Archives/Archive Photos/Getty Images; p. 35 (bottom) NARINDER NANU/AFP/Getty Images; p. 36 New York Daily News Archive/Getty Images; p. 38 Time Life Pictures/The LIFE Pucture Collection/Getty Images; p. 39 (top) Bettmann/Getty Images; p. 39 (bottom) Margaret Bourke-White/The LIFE Picture Collection/Getty Images; p. 41 (top) FAROOQ NAEEM/AFP/Getty Images; p. 41 (bottom) Rolls Press/Popperfoto/Getty Images; p. 42 DIBYANGSHU SARKAR/AFP/Getty Images; p. 43 Chris Hondros/Getty Images News/Getty Images; p. 44 PRAKASH MATHEMA/AFP/Getty Images; p. 45 (top) Tristo/Getty Images News/Getty Images; p. 45 (bottom) CORNELIUS POPPE/AFP/Getty Images News.

Cataloging-in-Publication Data
Names: Morlock, Rachael.
Title: The history and government of South Asia / Rachael Morlock.
Description: New York : PowerKids Press, 2021. | Series: One world | Includes glossary and index.
Identifiers: ISBN 9781725321403 (pbk.) | ISBN 9781725321427 (library bound) | ISBN 9781725321410 (6 pack) | ISBN 9781725321434 (ebook)
Subjects: LCSH: South Asia–Juvenile literature. | South Asia–History–Juvenile literature.| South Asia–Politics and government–Juvenile literature.
Classification: LCC DS340.M667 2021 | DDC 954–dc23

Manufactured in the United States of America

CPSIA Compliance Information: Batch #CSPK20: For Further Information contact Rosen Publishing, New York, New York at 1-800-237-9932

Find us on

CONTENTS

Introduction

SOUTH ASIA

The countries of South Asia are bordered by the impressive Himalayan Mountains to the north and the vast Indian Ocean to the south. This striking landscape is one of the natural barriers that kept the region separate from its neighbors for thousands of years. Diverse ecosystems in and around the Himalayan Mountains provide a rich and fertile environment. This setting gave rise to early agricultural societies, and the region contains the ruins of one of the oldest and most complex ancient civilizations. As diverse cultural and **ethnic** groups migrated, or moved, across the mountains or seas to enter South Asia, new chapters were written in the history of the region.

diverse: Different or varied.

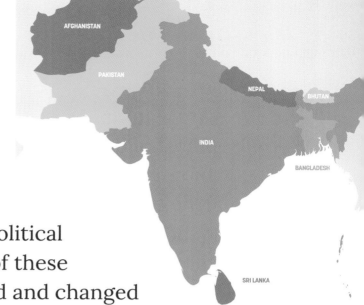

The countries of South Asia are often referred to as the Indian subcontinent. *That's because the countries are separated from the rest of the Asian continent, mainly by the Himalayan Mountains.*

Over time, the political boundaries of many of these countries have shifted and changed with waves of invasion, colonization, and independence. Three of the world's oldest religions were born here, and others took root. As a result, periods of peace and conflict between religions and world powers have shaped the region. These relationships have caused political and cultural movements that defined the major periods in South Asian history, from ancient to modern times. Today, this region is broken up into the nations of Afghanistan, Pakistan, India, Nepal, Bhutan, Bangladesh, Sri Lanka, and the Maldives. It is home to about 1.9 billion people.

subcontinent: A large landmass that is geographically set off from the larger continent.

colonization: The act of making or establishing a settlement in a new territory that maintains ties to a distant parent state.

Chapter One

ANCIENT CIVILIZATIONS

One of the earliest known settlements in South Asia is called Mehrgarh. It was a farming community established around 7000 BC in the area known today as Balochistan, Pakistan. The people of Mehrgarh grew barley and wheat, raised cattle, and made pottery. Over time, they expanded east toward the Indus Valley. The pre-Harappan culture developed in that area around 4000 BC. Like the Mehrgarh, pre-Harappans farmed the land. They grew peas, sesame seeds, dates, and cotton, and raised water buffalo. Trade with other regional groups allowed the culture to grow, which eventually gave rise to the Indus Valley civilization.

Sun-dried mud bricks were used to construct wells and storage units for farmed grains like barley and wheat. The Mehrgarh settlements were revealed after a flood in the 1970s.

Life and culture along the Indus River Valley developed into one of the most advanced ancient civilizations in the world. Every year, the Indus River flooded and deposited mineral-rich silt in the area. This silt created fertile land for farming. As a surplus of food was grown, it became possible to expand the functions of society and develop a unified culture. The Indus Valley Civilization reached its height around 2600 BC. At this time, it had developed organized cities, trade patterns, art, language, and technology. Over 1,000 cities and settlements were built along the Indus River,

silt: A rich soil deposited by rivers.

creating a culture of about 5 million people. Besides dominating, or controlling, the South Asian region, the Indus civilization's influence also reached westward through trade with Mesopotamia.

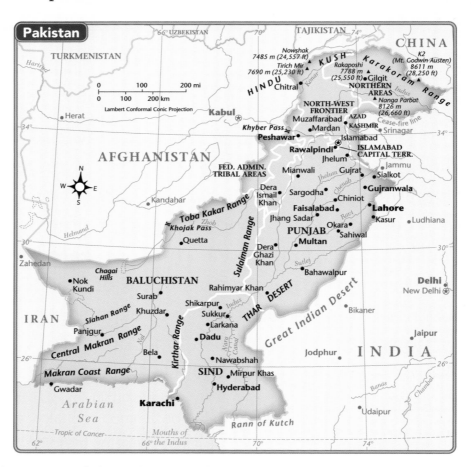

The source of the Indus River lies in modern-day China. The river runs through deep Himalayan gorges in northern India and Pakistan. Then, it flows south through Pakistan to the Arabian Sea.

ACHIEVEMENTS OF THE INDUS CIVILIZATION

The Indus Valley Civilization produced remarkable cultural achievements, which are visible in the remains of Mohenjo Daro and Harappa. Archaeologists rediscovered these well-organized cities in the 1920s. Urban planning is demonstrated in the grid-like arrangement of streets and equal access to water and drainage throughout the city. Indus art took shape in pottery, realistic sculpture, and seals. A distinct language was also part of the culture, although it has yet to be **deciphered**. Agriculture thrived outside the cities because of farm technology like plows, and **reservoirs** collected yearly monsoon rains. Some experts believe the civilization was also mainly peaceful—no signs of major conflict or an army have been uncovered.

The Indus civilization created a system of measurement that allowed them to excel in architecture and engineering. Indus people constructed buildings and wells—like the one seen here in Harappa—from uniform bricks.

History in F◉CUS

Social equality seems to be a main feature of the Indus civilization. No evidence of kings or slaves have been found, and all city houses had equal access to water and sewage.

monsoon: Seasonal winds that affect climate in the southern areas of Asia, resulting in wet spring and summer months and dry winter months.

Carved stone seals from the Indus civilization contained written symbols and animal images. One purpose of seals was economic. They were pressed into clay in order to seal containers and mark tags for traded goods.

After 1900 BC, the mighty Indus civilization began to decline. People moved eastward, and within 100 years many cities were deserted. Historians look to environmental changes for the cause. As the regional climate became cooler and drier, farming, herding, and hunting were more difficult. Many Indus peoples moved east in small groups into the Indo-Gangetic Plain in search of better farmland and food.

History in F⦿CUS

Historians have found little evidence to explain the decline of the Indus Valley Civilization. Some blame extreme flooding, changes in nearby river systems, and earthquakes, among other natural factors.

Indo-Gangetic Plain: A plain of fertile land along the Indus and Ganges Rivers in the northern part of the Indian subcontinent.

earthquake: A shaking of Earth's surface caused by the movement of large pieces of land called plates that run into each other.

The remains of a giant bath were found at Mohenjo Daro in modern-day Pakistan. Bathing is thought to have had a ceremonial importance in the culture. It may have influenced the ritual bathing practices of modern Hinduism.

Around the same time, a new community migrated to South Asia. People speaking Indo-European languages crossed the Hindu Kush mountains in Afghanistan and Pakistan to enter the region. Around 1500 BC, these Aryan people brought new languages, cultures, and traditions that blended with those native to the area. The resulting mixed culture formed the foundation of many of the languages and religious traditions that survive in South Asia today.

ARYAN MIGRATION

The Aryans were a group of nomads who **migrated** from Central Asia into the Indian subcontinent in large numbers. As they entered the Indus Valley and spread south and east across India, their culture merged with regional lifestyles. Aryans had shifted from nomadic to agricultural practices by 1000 BC. Their culture and language, Sanskrit, came to dominate the region. A new historic era of Vedic civilization developed from the blending cultures. The Vedas were important religious stories passed down orally, or by word of mouth, and they recorded ideas and events from this period. The stories were eventually written in Sanskrit, and today they provide clues about the growth of Aryan culture in South Asia.

Natural passes in the Hindu Kush mountains made it possible for Indo-Aryans to enter the Indian subcontinent. Their migration continued along the Indus River Valley and eastward into modern-day India.

migrate: To move from one region to another.

Chapter Two

KINGDOMS AND EMPIRES

After the migration of Aryans into South Asia, the history of the region was defined by a number of kingdoms and empires. Aryans and the Vedic civilization maintained dominance in the plains of northern India from about 1500 to 500 BC. They cultivated the land, built towns, and established trade along the Ganges River.

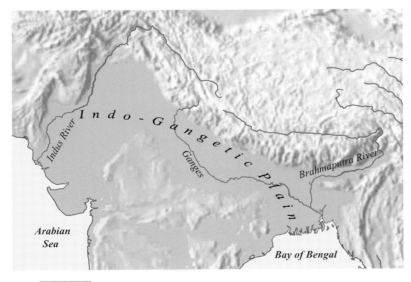

Indo-Gangetic Plain

Indus River

Ganges

Brahmaputra River

Arabian Sea

Bay of Bengal

The Indo-Gangetic Plain is the region south of the Himalayan Mountains that is watered by the Indus and Ganges River. Aryan migrants created farms and settlements in these fertile areas.

empire: A large territory controlled by one ruler.

As the population grew, a collection of tribes was established from Afghanistan in the west to Bangladesh in the east. The 16 Mahajanapadas, or "great kingdoms," were early republics. Councils of elders and assemblies made up from members of prominent, or important, family clans governed the republics. An elder was selected to rule, and his kingship was passed down through family lines. The political order organized trade, collected taxes, and offered military protection.

Kanchi Kailasanathar Temple in Kanchipuram, Tamil Nadu, is one of the oldest Hindu temples in India. The temple was constructed around the seventh century to honor the Hindu god Shiva.

republic: A form of government in which people elect representatives to legislate.

RISE OF RELIGIONS

South Asia is the birthplace of three major religions. Hinduism emerged from the beliefs and rituals of the Vedic civilization. Hindus worship a range of gods through rituals and prayers at temples. Buddhism came about in the sixth century BC through the teachings of Siddhartha Gautama, or Buddha. Buddhists focus on achieving inner peace through nonviolence, meditation, and moral acts. Around the same time as Buddhism, Jainism emerged from South Asia. Jains also practice nonviolence, meditation, and simple lifestyles. They teach that all living things have a soul. All three religions believe in the return of the soul through **reincarnation**.

A giant statue of Buddha sits in Bodh Gaya, the city in Bihar, India, where the Buddha is said to have achieved enlightenment while meditating under a tree.

As the Mahajanapadas struggled along their borders for power over each other, one kingdom eventually gained control. Chandragupta Maurya, an orphan who rose to power, led the Magadha kingdom to power and established the Mauryan Empire, which ruled over northern India from 326 to 184 BC. The empire functioned as a highly centralized government that oversaw taxes, trade, public spaces, and a large army. The government was **hierarchical** and divided its large territory into provinces, districts, and villages that were regulated by local officials.

The Mauryan Empire was one of the largest to rule the Indian subcontinent. The Mauryan emperor Ashoka had this Buddhist stupa in Sanchi, India, built in the third century BC. It was later enlarged.

centralized government: A government in which the most power is held by a small, organized group.

stupa: A Buddhist temple.

History in F◉CUS

Alexander the Great divided his troops as they entered the Hindu Kush in the summer of 327 BC. His armies conquered parts of Afghanistan and Pakistan. In 326 BC he fought Indian troops and established two cities before returning to Macedonia.

The Mauryan Empire declined after the death of its third ruler, Ashoka. In its place, local communities and forces exerted their control. Foreign groups also came to the northwest part of the region from Greece and Central Asia. In the south, the Satavahana dynasty ruled through the power of local chieftains beginning around 100 BC. It served as an important social, cultural, and commercial link between the northern and southern parts of the Indian subcontinent. Other ancient powers in southern India include the Tamil kingdoms of Chera, Chola, and Pandya.

dynasty: A line of rulers who belong to the same family.

ASHOKA THE GREAT

In 265 BC, Chandragupta Maurya's grandson, Ashoka, came to power. He governed the Mauryan Empire until 238 BC and was largely responsible for the spread of Buddhism across South Asia. After a bloody military campaign, Ashoka turned away from conflict and embraced the nonviolence of Buddhism. He allowed different religions and languages to flourish within the Mauryan Empire and maintained a peaceful rule that valued honesty, compassion, and reason over force. Ashoka oversaw the creation of public works like hospitals and wells. He also supported Buddhism by building stupas and sending Buddhist **missionaries** to Sri Lanka, where the religion flourished.

Ashoka recorded Buddhist ideals on inscribed pillars that were transported around the region. His messages were intended to inspire and guide believers. This Ashoka pillar still stands near a stupa in Vaishali, Bihar, India.

missionary: Someone who travels to a new place to spread their faith.

The Gupta Empire in northern India sparked some of the greatest achievements of South Asian history. From AD 320 to 550, Hindu religion and culture were nourished by the empire. Scientific, medical, and artistic advances surged, especially in the capital of Pataliputra. These trends continued to spread south after the Gupta Empire fell. After the year AD 650, the empire was replaced by smaller local governments that were often in conflict with each other.

History in F◉CUS

The reign of the Gupta Empire is known as the Golden Age of Indian history. Architects built Hindu temples, writers composed verses in Sanskrit, and scholars explored math and astronomy.

This coin was created around AD 400 during the reign of Chandragupta II, the third great Gupta ruler. The Gupta Empire declined after 230 years due to poor leadership and northern invasions.

Chapter Three

ISLAMIC INFLUENCES

The religion of Islam began in the sixth century AD in what is today's Saudi Arabia. After its founding, the Muslim community began to grow in Arab lands and beyond. The first Muslims to enter South Asia were merchants who followed trade routes across the subcontinent. Traders and migrants slowly began to spread across the region, due in part to the Silk Road trading network that passed through South Asia.

Silk Road: A historic trade route between China and Europe.

THE ISLAMIC FAITH

Muslims follow divine teachings from the prophet Muhammad. These teachings are recorded in the Qur'an, the religion's main holy text. In the Islamic tradition, the contents of the Qur'an were transmitted to Muhammad by the angel Gabriel from AD 610 to 632. Since then, Muhammad's followers have used the Qur'an as a guide to a pious, or religious, life. Muslims believe there is only one god and that Muhammad was the last prophet. They also follow the Five Pillars of Islam, teachings and practices that govern daily life for Muslims. The **polytheism** of indigenous religions in South Asia conflicted with the core beliefs of Islam.

In AD 711, a group of Muslims led by Muhammad bin Qãsim organized an attack on the southwestern coast of modern-day Pakistan. The Muslims were victorious, and they settled in the conquered territories of Sindh and Multan. After this first Arab conquest, more Muslims began arriving along the western coast of the Indian subcontinent. In the 10th and 11th centuries, Muslims from Central Asia crossed the Hindu Kush mountains to enter the region and conquer northern lands.

indigenous: Describing groups that are native to a particular region.

Buddhists built the Nalanda monastery in the fifth century. Muslims from the Ghurid Empire attacked it in 1197. This event signaled the decline of Buddhism in India.

These military conquests in northern India led to the creation of the Delhi Sultanate, which ruled from 1206 to 1526. A sultanate is a government run by a sultan, or a Muslim king. Five distinct dynasties and their kings passed down control of the Delhi Sultanate over the course of more than 300 years. Other sultanates were created and dissolved in central and southern India, like the Bahmani Sultanate. Overall, the most southern regions of India remained under the control of Hindu kingdoms.

monastery: A religious community where monks live and work together.

The Qutb Minar is a minaret, or tall tower, that's used to call Muslims to prayer. It was built in 1225 under the Delhi Sultanate and it's the world's tallest minaret made of bricks.

VIJAYNAGAR EMPIRE

Although Islamic powers reigned in the north, southern India was largely independent from Muslim rulers. The Vijaynagar Empire was the last great Hindu empire in India. The empire grew and prospered from 1336 until 1614, and it managed to remain beyond the reach of Mughal expansion. One of its most notable leaders was Krishnadevaraya, who built Hindu temples and encouraged artistic growth from 1509 to 1529. Although Vijaynagar was not controlled by Muslim rulers, it did benefit from cultural exchange with Muslim writers, poets, and artists. The empire declined slowly, and by 1646 was replaced with small dynasties.

Large palaces, temples, and gateways demonstrated the wealth and artistry of the Vijaynagar empire. In 1565, the capital city was toppled in a battle with Muslim forces. Its ruins survive in Hampi, Karnataka, India.

The greatest period of Muslim rule occurred under the Mughal Dynasty. Beginning in 1526, descendants of Ghengis Khan and the Mongol Empire crossed the Khyber Pass in modern-day Afghanistan and began building an empire. Over the course of three hundred years, three important emperors—Babur, Akbar, and Aurangzeb—collected Mughal territories and subjects through military campaigns.

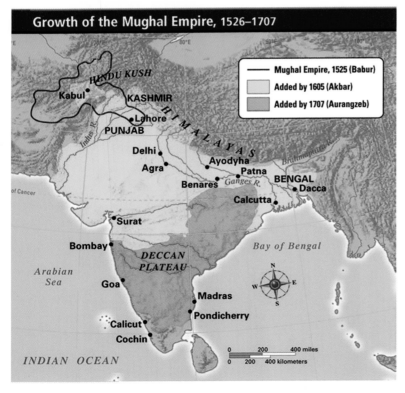

Growth of the Mughal Empire, 1526–1707

— Mughal Empire, 1525 (Babur)
Added by 1605 (Akbar)
Added by 1707 (Aurangzeb)

This map shows how emperors Babur, Akbar, and Aurangzeb expanded Mughal territories over the course of three centuries. The Mughal Empire maintained control by incorporating Indian leaders into the power structure of the empire.

The Mughal Empire centralized Muslim power across India and established organized government practices. The Mughals brought Persian art and culture to the area, and their Persian language mixed with Hindi and Arabic to form Urdu. Today, Urdu is the official language of Pakistan, and widely spoken in India.

Emperors Babur and Akbar promoted a degree of religious tolerance in the region. They integrated Hindu princes and politicians into political and military structures in a way that strengthened and united the vast and diverse people of the empire.

Emperor Akbar is shown in this 16th century painting conversing with Jesuit missionaries. In 1575, Akbar established a meeting place in Fatehpur Sikri for people of all religious backgrounds to share and discuss their beliefs.

History in F☉CUS

Tombs in South Asia, like the Taj Mahal, are directly tied to the rise of Islam. Indigenous people cremated, or burned, their dead. Therefore, the tombs and mosques built in the region demonstrate the influence of Islam.

Jesuit: A member of a Roman Catholic religious order that is officially called the Society of Jesus. It was founded in 1534 by St. Ignatius Loyola.

mosque: A building that is used for Muslim religious services.

The Taj Mahal was built in Agra, India, between 1631 and 1648 by the Mughal emperor Shah Jahan. The impressive structure is a tomb for Shah Jahan's wife.

When Emperor Aurangzeb came to power in 1658, his approach was less open-minded and more intolerant. For example, he made non-Muslims pay a poll tax, or jizya. After his death in 1707, the Mughal Empire was weakened until its end in 1857.

Chapter Four

BRITISH RULE

European powers began to explore trade opportunities in South Asia in the 15th century. In 1498, the Portuguese established their presence in the subcontinent with trading posts on the western coast. By 1505, they had also established control in parts of Sri Lanka. Their 1510 victory in Goa, India, secured Portuguese power over the spice trade until the rise of the British East India Company in the 1600s. This company slowly began to exert control over the region. By 1757, it was on its way to ruling most of the subcontinent.

History in FOCUS

Because of British colonization of South Asia, English is often spoken there. Other languages in the region include Urdu, Pashtun, and Hindi.

From 1757 to 1857, the British East India Company engaged in violent military campaigns on the Indian subcontinent. They sought to expand company territory and access local goods like spices, cotton, and opium. The Battle of Plassey in 1757 and the Battle of Buxar in 1764 established British control over much of Northern India. Campaigns through the 19th century acquired even more land to the west. In addition to military tactics, the British collaborated with local leaders in order to assert British control. They made agreements, called *sanad*, that divided governing powers between the company and local leaders. As a result, princely states emerged in India in which territories were governed by regional princes but under the umbrella of British rule.

This artwork from 1820 shows men from the British East India Company being welcomed by a local Indian community. The British East India Company was created in 1600 to establish a trading network across continents.

opium: A bitter, addictive drug derived from the fruit of opium poppies.

History in F✺CUS

British rule in India was made possible by the collaboration of local South Asian leaders. Over a third of British territories were run by Indian princes who gave power to the British to avoid conflict and maintain some control.

British parliament passed a series of laws and acts designed to aid the British East India Company in reforming the Indian subcontinent. They viewed many of the cultural and religious practices of South Asia as morally or socially inferior to British practices. In addition, British interests began spreading the English language and modernizing the region with railroads and transportation routes, telegraph lines, and a

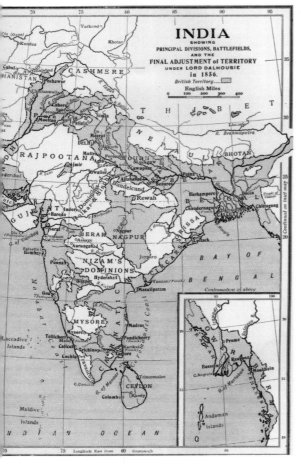

This map illustrates British colonization of India in 1856. Areas of direct British rule were gained through military campaigns. Most of the remaining Indian territories were ruled indirectly through princely states.

unified postal service. Some Indian people worried about Westernization, including the possible breakdown of the traditional Indian caste system.

This artwork from 1842 shows British troops in their failed attempt to occupy Afghanistan. Only one British soldier was spared when Afghan forces ambushed, or sneak-attacked, the retreating British troops.

FIRST AFGHAN WAR

While the British were conquering South Asia, Russia was gaining control of Central Asia. British and Russian interests collided in Afghanistan, the bridge between the two regions. The British fought the First Afghan War from 1838 to 1842 to create a barrier to Russian expansion and set up an allied Muslim ruler. With the help of Indian and Sikh soldiers, the British conquered the cities of Kandahar and Kabul. Despite this victory, they were unable to maintain control of the cities and soon admitted defeat. As British troops made their way back through the mountains toward India, Afghans attacked. They left only one British soldier alive.

caste system: A system that separates people based on heredity and limits social groups to people of similar rank, occupation, and economic status.

Westernization: Conversion to or adoption of traditions or techniques of western cultures.

A rebellion in 1857 by Indian members of the British army called sepoys triggered a shift in power. The rebels surrendered in 1858 after bloody conflict. To prevent future uprisings, the British territories in the subcontinent came under the direct control of the British monarchy. The British-Indian government was reconstructed under the authority of the governor-general, or viceroy. Provincial governors functioned beneath the viceroy, and district officials oversaw the next level

History in F☉CUS

The Sepoy Rebellion of 1857 is also called India's First War of Independence. Sepoys revolted against the British and offered allegiance to the Mughal emperor in Delhi. The British exiled the emperor in response, marking the end of the Mughal Empire.

Sepoys felt that the British did not respect their religions and customs. Both Hindu and Muslim sepoys were upset by a rumor that gun cartridges were greased with animal fat, which made them break religious laws.

allegiance: Support of a country, group, or cause.

of government. British-born citizens filled positions in each level. To combat this injustice, Indians began organizing their quest for political power.

Queen Victoria of England was named the Empress of India on January 1, 1877. Victoria promised her new subjects religious freedom, education, participation in government, and equal rights with British citizens.

FAMINES

From 1857 to 1900, 25 famines struck the Indian subcontinent while it was under British rule. Between 30 and 40 million people died in food shortages related to weather patterns and colonial policies. Many Indians were unable to adapt when **drought** or flooding threatened crops, because British laws had restricted, or limited, access to local farmland. Laws also limited trade, taxed residents, drove inflation, and sent food to England. These changes and restrictions added to the environmental challenges of the region and left millions hungry. Many Indians reacted to the famines by pushing harder for political equality and self-governance.

The Great Famine of 1876 to 1878 claimed the lives of about 5.5 million people in India. In this image, children in southern India struggle to prepare food for their cattle.

Chapter Five

INDEPENDENCE MOVEMENTS

After 1858, Indians increasingly called for a larger role in the government. But British legislation only minimally extended the political rights of Indians. Unsatisfied with their progress, a group of educated, upper-class Indians created the Indian National Congress in 1885. The policies and reforms promoted by the Congress left many Muslims feeling **isolated**. To protect Islamic identity in India, they formed the Muslim League in 1906. Over the next few decades, these two nationalist movements overlapped and disagreed at turns.

World War I (1914–1918) sent over 1 million Indian soldiers into battle, killing more than 74,000. When soldiers returned from war, they

nationalist: Supporting national independence.

were disappointed to find that their service failed to earn them greater rights at home. The reality of continued **oppression** was highlighted by the Rowlatt Act of 1919, which stripped Indians of their rights to organize politically. The Jallianwala Bagh Massacre on April 13, 1919, further fueled the struggle for independence.

Indian soldiers serving on the front lines in France later returned to a life of reduced rights and political oppression in India. About 74,000 Indian soldiers died during World War I.

History in F◉CUS

In April 1919, about 10,000 people gathered in Amritsar, India, to celebrate a Sikh holiday. British soldiers opened fire on the group, killing close to 400 Sikhs and wounding more in the Jallianwala Bagh Massacre.

Women pay their respects and examine the bullet holes left behind at the site of the Jallianwala Bagh Massacre. Soldiers shot into an unarmed crowd during the massacre.

In response to oppressive actions and laws, Mohandas Karamchand Gandhi led a series of large-scale marches, protests, and boycotts across India beginning in 1920. These movements were nonviolent **retaliations** against British rule. One of the largest movements was the Salt March. From March 12th to April 6th, 1930, the march covered about 250 miles (402 km). Gandhi and thousands of followers ended their march by collecting salt from the sea—a symbolic act against British laws and taxes on salt.

Mohandas Gandhi (called Mahatma Gandhi), center, and tens of thousands of followers made a seaward journey through India on foot. By illegally gathering salt from the sea, they protested the right of the British to hold a **monopoly** on Indian goods.

GANDHI'S NONVIOLENT REVOLUTION

Gandhi encouraged the practice of ahimsa, or nonviolence. He was convinced that noncooperation with British rulers could bring about change for India. Gandhi encouraged Indians to boycott all British goods and institutions, including textiles, schools, courts, elections, and taxes. He focused on **self-sufficiency** and using only Indian-made goods. For example, he spun cotton to make his own clothes and avoid British products. Gandhi also led large, public acts of resistance like the Salt March. In 1942, he initiated the "Quit India Movement," which urged Britain to leave India immediately. Gandhi was imprisoned several times for his role in protests that were both powerful and effective.

Although Gandhi hoped to unify the Hindu and Muslim communities of India, the Muslim League followed a separate path. Muslims increasingly feared the establishment of a Hindu-majority government after independence. Muhammad Ali Jinnah led the campaign for the creation of a Muslim state instead. In 1940, Jinnah supported the call for an independent Islamic nation named Pakistan.

The Indian National Congress, captured in this image from the 1930s, also included female members. Women were encouraged to participate alongside men in the Indian nationalist movement.

World War II (1939–1945) finally sparked the changes Indian nationalists had been working toward. War exhausted British resources and convinced the empire that India was more trouble than it was worth. The Indian Independence Act was passed in 1947, ending colonial rule. Then the British organized a rapid withdrawal from the subcontinent and established a partition that divided the land into Muslim and Hindu nations. India was sandwiched in the middle between the new areas of East Pakistan and West Pakistan.

THE INDIAN PARTITION

The creation of separate Islamic and Hindu nations by the Indian partition ignited a period of great migration. Over 10 million people relocated, or moved, to join the new nations. Muslims in India moved to Pakistan, and Hindus in Pakistan moved to India. Their movements created the Muslim majorities in Pakistan and Bangladesh that persist today, and the Hindu majority in India. Although independence had been achieved, cultural struggles continued. Over 1 million people were killed in the mass migrations, and Sikhs were especially targeted by violence. The partition also created lasting zones of conflict, especially in the Kashmir region of the Indian subcontinent.

partition: A division.

Jawaharlal Nehru, on the left, became the first prime minister of independent India, serving from 1947 to 1964. He's seen here with Muhammad Ali Jinnah, the leader of the Muslim League.

History in F⊙CUS

Three wars have been fought between India and Pakistan since the partition. During the last war in 1971, East Pakistan was dissolved and Bangladesh emerged as an independent nation.

After centuries of living in mixed communities, the partition of India sought to separate religious groups. In addition to Hindus and Muslims, Sikhs formed a portion of the millions of people migrating between India and Pakistan.

Chapter Six

DEMOCRACY IN SOUTH ASIA

The nations and governments of South Asia have continued to change since the end of British colonialism. The countries have used their independence to structure diverse forms of government. However, all of these nations have suffered from political instability and violence. Civil wars dominated the recent histories of Afghanistan, Sri Lanka, and Nepal, in addition to the Pakistani civil war that created Bangladesh. Political coup d'états have toppled leaders. Military rule has also been common throughout the region. Despite these challenges, all of today's South Asian governments practice varying forms of democracy.

coup d'état: A sudden attempt by a small group of people to take over the government, usually through violence.

democracy: A system of government whereby people choose leaders and participate in making laws through an election process.

The flags of all eight South Asian countries mark a meeting of the South Asian Association for Regional Cooperation (SAARC), a collaborative organization designed to advance the social and economic growth of the region.

History in F◉CUS

In 1971, a civil war broke out between East and West Pakistan. East Pakistan sought greater self-government. The war ended when East Pakistan became the independent nation of Bangladesh.

Amir Abdullah Khan Niazi, general of the Pakistan Army, is seen on the right as he prepares to sign the surrender documents that ended the Bangladesh Liberation War in 1971. The war resulted in the independent nation of Bangladesh.

India, Pakistan, Bangladesh, and Nepal are federal republics, or federal parliamentary republics. They're made up of a federation of states with a balance of state and federal power. As parliamentary republics, the legislative and

federal republic: A political arrangement in which states agree to form a national government to cooperate on matters of common interest.

executive branches of their governments are joined. Members of parliament are elected by the public. They make laws and select the prime minister. All four countries are led by a prime minister as head of the government and a president as head of the state.

WORLD'S LARGEST DEMOCRACY

After independence, India modeled its government on the British parliamentary system. The Indian Constitution went into effect in 1950. It outlines the structure of a parliamentary republic with a House of the People, prime minister, cabinet, a Council of States, and a mainly ceremonial president. From the early days of Indian independence, the Congress Party and Jawarhalal Nehru's family were dominant forces in Indian government. More recently, multiple parties have exerted their influence over Indian politics. All adult citizens in India have the right to vote, and India's huge population makes it the largest democracy in the world.

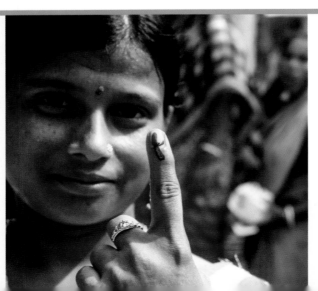

On election day, a woman in India shows off the ink mark on her finger which indicates that she voted. Over 67 percent of qualifying Indians voted in the 2019 election.

History in F◉CUS

The Maldives and Sri Lanka are presidential republics. The president is elected directly by the people every five years. Similarly, Afghanistan is a presidential Islamic republic. That means that the national laws of Afghanistan must agree with the laws of Islamic practice. An extreme Muslim group called the Taliban held power in Afghanistan from 1996 until the United States invaded in 2001. The United States toppled the Taliban in their search for terrorists, and supported the institution of a democratic government. The first election of the new democracy was held in 2004, though democratic practices in the region remain unstable.

Violence and unrest have forced **refugees** *out of Afghanistan for 40 years. The 1979 Soviet Union invasion and strict Taliban laws have pushed many Afghans, like the students shown here, into refugee camps in Pakistan.*

History in F⬤CUS

From 1983 to 2009, Sri Lanka was the site of a brutal and bloody civil war. The war resulted from ethnic tension between Tamil and Sinhalese groups on the island.

Monarchy was once the most common form of rule in South Asia. The monarchy of Afghanistan ended in 1979. A long history of monarchs ruled the government of Nepal from 1846 until 2008. Today, Bhutan is South Asia's last surviving monarchy, following the form of a constitutional monarchy. The constitution describes the rights, duties, and responsibilities the monarch must follow in order to maintain their position.

*The monarchy of Nepal began to decline in the 1990s as **communist** ideas spread in the country. In 2008, the monarchy ended and Ram Baran Yadav become the first president of Nepal.*

For Bhutan and all countries of the region, democracy promotes the participation of South Asian people in their own government. This gives them more power in determining the social, cultural, economic, and political advances of the future of South Asia.

constitutional monarchy: A system of government in which a country is ruled by a monarch whose power is limited by a constitution.

THE KINGDOM OF BHUTAN

Despite Tibetan invasions, border conflicts, and its brief designation as a British protectorate, the country of Bhutan was never colonized. In 1907, Bhutan became a monarchy when it named Sir Ugyen Wangchuck its first king. Bhutan's first constitution was written in 2005. It details the roles of a national council, a national assembly, and the monarch.

In the past few decades, Bhutan has lightened its general policy of separation from the outside world. However, Bhutan forced people with Nepalese heritage out of the country in the 1990s. This created a difficult refugee situation throughout the region and strained relations between Bhutan and the international community.

Jigme Khesar Namgyel Wangchuck became the fifth "Dragon King," or the king of Bhutan, in 2008. He and his wife, Queen Jetsun Pema, were married in 2011.

Malala Yousafzai accepts the Nobel Peace Prize in 2014. Yousafzai was shot by the Taliban in her home country of Pakistan on her way to school. Today, she fights for education for girls around the world.

History in F⊙CUS

The COVID-19 global pandemic, which started in 2019, put stress on governments in this region and around the world that will continue to have lasting effects.

protectorate: A state that is controlled and protected by another.

GLOSSARY

communist: Referring to a way of organizing society where there is no privately owned property.

decipher: To change into an understandable form.

drought: A long period of very dry weather.

ethnic: Having to do with a group that shares common cultural traits, such as language.

hierarchical: Describing a system that places people in a series of levels with varying importance or status.

isolated: Set apart.

monopoly: A situation in which only one company controls an industry or product.

oppression: The unjust use of power over another; treating people in a cruel or unfair way.

polytheism: A belief in many gods.

refugee: A migrant person who flees their homeland to escape disaster, persecution, or war.

reincarnation: Rebirth into new forms of life.

reservoir: A usually man-made lake where water is stored.

retaliation: The act of striking back.

self-sufficiency: The ability to take care of oneself without outside help.